Control isn't power;
it's fear. Real power
is letting go.

D0734836

An attitude of gratitude

creates blessings.

—Sir John Templeton

Words of Gratitude

FOR MIND, BODY, AND SOUL

Robert A. Emmons and Joanna Hill

Introduction by Brother David Steindl-Rast

MJF BOOKS
NEW YORK

Published by MJF Books

Fine Communications

322 Eighth Avenue

New York, NY 10001

Words of Gratitude for Mind, Body, and Soul

LC Control Number 2006940265

ISBN-13: 978-1-56731-853-1

ISBN-10: 1-56731-853-3

This edition is published by MJF Books

in arrangement with Templeton Foundation Press.

Printed in the United States of America.

MJF Books and the MJF colophon are trademarks of Fine Creative Media, Inc.

VB 10 9 8 7 6 5 4 3 2 1

CONTENTS

WORDS OF GRATITUDE

for Mind, Body, and Soul

Love wholeheartedly,
be surprised,
give thanks and praise—
then you will
discover the fullness
of your life.

—Brother David Steindl-Rast

INTRODUCTION:
PROVERBS AS WORDS OF GRATITUDE

Brother David Steindl-Rast

A Chinese proverb popped into my mind the moment I read the opening question of this book, "What is gratitude?" The proverb answers: *When you drink from a stream, remember the spring.* Remember! Be mindful! Think! Thinking and thanking spring from the same root—in the realm of language as well as in the soul realm. Only the thoughtful are thankful. Our proverb caught it all in one image: remembering the spring as we drink from the source; this is gratitude.

Suddenly I realized that one important place to look for words of gratitude is among the world's proverbs. Gratitude runs as an undercurrent throughout human experience at its most vibrant, always and everywhere. Age after age we humans have harvested the fruit of experience as perennial wisdom and distilled its essence into proverbs. *Proverbs are the daughters of experience* (Dutch). No wonder that they tell us much about gratitude, much that reflects and confirms the insights of this book.

My childhood culture in Austria—between the two World Wars—still agreed with the Tatars for whom *Proverbs are the jewelry of speech,* or the African Yoruba, for whom *A proverb is the horse of conversation.* My uncles, whose every other sentence was a proverb, rode that horse gallantly. But in our postmodern world, proverbs are an endangered species. One specimen that has survived happens to deal with gratitude: *Never look a gift horse in the mouth.*

Today's way of dealing with the topic of gratitude must be more sophisticated than proverbs; our time is self-conscious, reflective, rational, analytic. The two authors of this book are eminently qualified to treat their topic in an up-to-date way. Robert A. Emmons has pioneered a strictly scientific study of gratitude and has achieved significant psychological and sociological results. Joanna Hill brings to her task a wide anthropological horizon and a refined spiritual sensitivity. It is all the more striking that their carefully reasoned insights match, point by point, the intuitive imagery of perennial wisdom that speaks in proverbs. *Though a proverb be abandoned, it is not falsified,* the Irish say.

This book offers us words of gratitude from many different cultures and historical periods, but it does more: it carries a message. Gratitude is here presented as more than a feeling, a virtue, or an experience; gratitude emerges as an attitude we can freely choose in order to create a better life for ourselves and for others. The Nigerian Hausa put it this way: *Give thanks for a little and you will find a lot.* The key to finding gifts wherever we look is in our own hands; the key is gratitude. *Count your blessings* and you will find them to be countless, even in the midst of adversity and tragic circumstances. *A lame foot is better than none.* Who can deny it? *Better eye sore than all blind.*

Proverbs are the coin of the common people (Russian), of the poor who have no other coins to count, who can only survive by counting their blessings. The hungry have come up with a thousand variations on the theme of this Ovambo proverb from Angola: *Hunger is a good cook. Hunger is the best sauce* (English). *When you are hungry, nothing is tasteless* (Japan). *Hunger turns beans into almonds* (Italian).

Beggars can't be choosers. But they can choose to be grateful, and they do so—more often, perhaps, than those who live in plenty. *The smallest fish is better than an empty dish. Better a crust than no bread at all.* Or, with some humor: *Better a louse in the pot than no meat at all.*

It moves me deeply to think that so many of the world's noblest words of gratitude have come down to us from the unwashed, nameless, homeless ones. *Better a bush than an open field*, they said, when they sought shelter for the night. And in the morning, stiff from the cold, they stretched their limbs and gratefully acknowledged: *The sun is the poor people's blanket.* Gratefulness creates solidarity with the poor throughout the world.

If we have eyes to look through deceptive trappings, we realize that we are all poor. *Naked we come into this world, naked we leave it;* the proverb paraphrases Job, the biblical archetype of one who is poor in a spiritual sense. Whatever we have is gift. To look up to the Source of all gifts makes us grateful; it distinguishes us from dumb beasts. *A hog never looks up to the one who threshes down the acorns.* What makes us truly human is gratefulness. *Better a grateful dog than an ungrateful human.*

By looking up, by raising our eyes above our limited horizon, we are more likely to perceive the blessings hidden in affliction. The delay of a gift may be as great a gift as the delayed gift itself. *Late spring: great blessing.* Gratefulness is not a state in which suffering and adversity are selectively ignored. Rather, gratefulness makes us focus on the opportunity that adversity offers, the opportunity of authentic spiritual growth. This turns suffering into growing pains. *A bitter winter brings a sweet summer.* If we dare to taste even the bitterness as a gift, it will bring about sweetness. We will find that *Not a single season is without fruit* (Turkish), and *Everything is good in its season* (Italian).

Many of the lines I am using in this Introduction to connect and parallel the proverbs are quotes and paraphrases from the book you are holding in hand. One of the most helpful features of this book is that it suggests methods for cultivating gratitude. A Polish proverb is skeptical in this respect. *Gratitude has gone to heaven and pulled up the ladder.* Yet, even this proverb implies two main contentions of Emmons and Hill: a ladder of gratitude exists and it leads to a heavenly state—if only we can retrieve that ladder. Retrieve it we can, by practicing step-by-step that gratitude which is the door to many heavenly gifts.

That door is low, however, and we must be humble to enter. Pride is one of the hindrances to gratitude, to which the authors devote a special chapter. *Pride and grace dwell never in one place.* The most harmful form of pride is our contemporary notion of entitlement. By considering every gift as ours by right, we set no limits to our wants, impoverishing our lives in the midst of abundance. *They are not poor that have little, but they that desire much. The richest man, whatever his lot, is the one who's content with whatever he's got* (Dutch); nothing causes content but gratitude. As a Turkish proverb says: *For the grateful, the gnats make music; for the ungrateful harps and flutes make only noise.*

A contented heart is a continual feast. Since those who know how to feast never lack company, gratitude brings people together in peace and harmony. Even rigorous clinical studies show that gratefulness tends to build and strengthen social bonds and friendships. *Gratefulness waters old friendships and makes new ones sprout* (Russian). *Gift giving binds friends together,* claims another Russian proverb; *Bound is he that takes a gift,* replies an English one. Yes, "bound," but by what bonds? By the very bonds that hold a healthy society together. Only fools flaunt their independence. To recognize the interdependence of all with all is true wisdom; to live by it is true contentment. The give-and-take of a grateful society thrives on what this Russian proverb counsels: *Speak when you receive; be silent when you give.*

People remind us of their gifts; God never reminds us. We have to remind ourselves to be mindful, to remember. The greatest gift is life itself. A Chinese proverb reminds us, tongue in cheek: *The poorest beggar will not cross a rotten bridge.* Still, one gift is greater than life: gratitude; for without gratitude we will not appreciate life. So the final chapter of this book deals with reminding ourselves of God's gifts, with praying for gratitude.

If we cannot pray from gratitude, we can pray to experience gratitude. To many people this comes quite spontaneously. For others it seems too much like "talking to someone up there." Yet, "God isn't someone else," as Thomas Merton expressed a universal mystical insight. To live our innermost truth with integrity is gratefulness; it is the full response to what is gratuitously given—namely, everything. Our very existence is a "given" fact; what we mindfully make of it is our gratitude-in-action.

Washing the dishes, writing a memo, mowing the lawn—all can be acts of gratitude. Still, many people find it helpful to perform some simple gesture that is *nothing but* an expression of gratitude. The website www.gratefulness.org offers the simple ritual of lighting a candle in cyberspace. Statistics show that amazing numbers of people avail themselves of this opportunity. Obviously, there is a need in many hearts to express without words the desire to be grateful, to remember. Here we come back to the image with which we began, *When you drink from the stream, remember the spring*.

This book itself resembles a mountain stream whose water sparkles in the sunlight. Reading it, we feel refreshed by the words of gratitude that flow through these pages and remember that they arose from the currents of many traditions fed by the never-failing Spring deep in the human heart. This book is a gift for which I myself am deeply grateful.

*To be grateful is to recognize the Love of God
in everything He has given us—and He has given
us everything. Every breath we draw is a gift of His love,
every moment of existence is a grace, for it brings with it
immense graces from Him. Gratitude therefore takes
nothing for granted, is never unresponsive, is constantly
awakening to new wonder and to praise of the goodness
of God. For the grateful person knows that God is good,
not by hearsay but by experience. And that is
what makes all the difference.*

—THOMAS MERTON

WHAT IS GRATITUDE?

ratitude is a sense of thankfulness and joy in response to receiving a gift—whether the gift be deserved or not, whether it is a concrete object or an abstract gesture of kindness. Gratitude can be a moment of at-oneness that is evoked in the presence of natural beauty or in the silence of the soul, a moment when the world—with both its abundance and its challenges—makes perfect sense, when its gifts can be seen and appreciated in whatever wrappings they come in.

Gratitude can also be a conscious, rational choice to focus on life's blessings rather than on its shortcomings; it can be

Eventually, when we look back on our existence,
we see it all as a blessing, so we thank God
for the fear, we thank God for the doubt,
we thank God for the anger.
And we thank God as each form of
negativity becomes unnecessary
as a response in our lives.

—JOHN MORTON

developed into a spiritual practice to create a positive outlook on life. It is a feeling, a moral attribute, a virtue, a mystical experience, and a conscious act, all in one. Gratitude is a universal human experience that can be either a random occurrence of grace or an attitude chosen to create a better life.

There are times that gratitude comes over us as a wave—lifting us higher than we can normally stand, then setting us back down on our feet after bringing us closer to God. At other times it is our companion during our darkest moments, causing us to be grateful for the good in the midst of tragedy, encouraging us to believe that good can come even when we cannot understand our own suffering or the suffering of others.

How we can learn to express and experience gratitude depends on our personal religious perspective, our psychological makeup, and our level of awareness. The process

We have to say simply,
"Lord, I receive, and I am grateful."
It doesn't matter what religion you practice;
we must all surrender to the highest source we can.
All of us must ask for protection,
for that is what surrender really is—
placing ourselves into the protecting hands of God.

—JOHN-ROGER

begins with awareness that we have a choice. The next step requires a necessary stillness within ourselves so we can do the internal work of being grateful. Then the feeling of gratitude becomes a conscious attitude and is expressed through our actions.

There is a paradoxical aspect to gratitude as well: the more grateful we are, the more reasons we have to be grateful. This knowledge can create a shift from gratitude as a response to gratitude as an attitude, as a receptive state that allows blessings to flow in. For a person who has religious or spiritual beliefs, this attitude brings about a relationship with the Divine, the source from which all good comes. We gratefully recognize that the gift of life comes from the Creator and respond with humility, awe, and recognition of how blessed we are to have the opportunity to learn, grow, love, create, share, and help others.

Gratitude unlocks the fullness of life.
It turns what we have into enough, and more.
It turns denial into acceptance,
chaos to order, confusion to clarity.
It can turn a meal into a feast, a house into a home,
a stranger into a friend.
Gratitude makes sense of our past, brings peace for today,
and creates a vision for tomorrow.

—MELODY BEATTIE

Gratitude becomes thanksgiving as we become aware of the benevolence of others. This recognition of good will creates a sense of connection and community and contradicts the sense of isolation and alienation that is the experience of many people. It moves us beyond self-sufficiency to an acknowledgment that we are connected to those around us—family, friends, and colleagues. This feeling of community can permeate everything we do; it can make us better people and can make the world a more peaceful and loving place in which to live.

How do we get there? Is gratitude one of those "unfair" gifts given to those of sunny dispositions, those who do not instinctively feel the anxiety, pain, and separation of living in this world? Is gratitude an emotion that comes from a chemical predisposition to optimism, or are there choices we can make? Can we choose gratitude?

[T]hose who are in internal things, that is to say those who have felt delight in benevolence and charity toward the neighbor, and above all those who have felt blessedness in love to the Lord, are encompassed with a grateful and pleasant sphere which is the heavenly sphere itself, and therefore they are in heaven.

—Emanuel Swedenborg

Emanuel Swedenborg, an eighteenth-century Swedish scientist and theologian, wrote that those who feel love toward the neighbor and a blessedness toward God are in a grateful sphere or heavenly state, and are thus in heaven. Therefore, gratitude enables us to live in a joyful, peaceful state; in its paradoxical, elusive way, gratitude is the door to many heavenly gifts. But the door is low, and we must humble ourselves to enter.

As we express gratitude, we recognize our relationship to the Creator who fills our lives with love and meaning as well as with tests and challenges—all help us grow to be wiser and more loving. Our response to these gifts can be an overwhelming sense of humility, wonder, and desire to give thanks and to pass along the love that has been activated within us. First we look up, then, out. We sense we are not separate from others or from God. And for this we are very grateful.

Give thanks for sorrow that teaches you pity;
for pain that teaches you courage—and give exceeding
thanks for the mystery, which remains a mystery still—
the veil that hides you from the infinite, which makes it
possible for you to believe in what you cannot see.

—ROBERT NATHAN

GRATITUDE THROUGH THE AGES

Teaching and developing gratitude are components of most religious traditions, from the ancients to modern spiritual-growth groups. Along with forgiveness and agape love, gratitude bridges a theological perspective with psychological understanding of human nature. A look at several traditions will demonstrate how gratitude is expressed; however, as a universal human experience, it can be found in all true religions. The sacred writings, prayers, and teachings of Judaism, Christianity, and Islam help us to see that giving thanks is a timeless way to express our relationship to the Divine. In the following sections, we will

Hear, O Israel: The Lord our God, the Lord is one.
And thou shalt love the Lord thy God with all thy heart,
and with all thy soul, and with all thy might.
And these words which I command thee this day,
shall be upon thy heart.
And thou shalt teach them diligently unto thy children,
and shalt talk of them when thou sittest in thy house, and
when thou walkest by the way, and when thou liest down,
and when thou risest up.
And thou shalt bind them for a sign upon thy hand,
and they shall be for frontlets between thine eyes. And thou
shalt write them upon the doorposts of thy house,
and upon thy gates.

—DEUTERONOMY 6:4–9

examine Buddhist practices of gratitude as well as ways of experiencing gratitude in our daily lives that are not derived from religious traditions.

JUDAISM

In Judaism, gratitude is a vital component of worship and permeates every aspect of the worshiper's daily life. In the Hebrew Scriptures, the poetry of the Psalms is saturated with thanksgiving to God: "O LORD my God, I will give thanks to you forever" (30:12) and "I will give thanks to the LORD with my whole heart" (9:1).

The day starts with the Shema, which begins: "You shall love the LORD your God with all your heart, and with all your soul, and with all your might" (Deuteronomy 6:5). The concluding prayer, the 'alenu, thanks God for the particular destiny of the Jewish people.

Say also:
"Save us, O God of our salvation,
And gather and rescue us from among the nations,
that we may give thanks to your holy name,
and glory in your praise.
Blessed be the Lord, the God of Israel,
From everlasting to everlasting."
Then all the people said "Amen!"
and praised the Lord.

—I CHRONICLES 16:35–36

Thankfulness for everything is appropriate in Judaism because all things come from God in the Hebrew worldview; therefore, Jewish life is filled with this recognition. A prayer is said upon hearing good or bad news, and God is praised for everything. In this way, a divine perspective on life is maintained.

CHRISTIANITY

Gratitude has always been central among Christian virtues and appears in classical and modern devotional writings as well as in the Old and New Testaments. In Christian gratitude, God is the giver of all gifts and the ultimate foundation for thankfulness. There is a feeling of indebtedness to the Creator, Sustainer, and Redeemer. God's generosity provides the model for how Christians are to deal with their own children and with each other.

*The reason why frankincense and incenses were used
in sacred rites among the ancients, is that odor
corresponds to perception, and a fragrant odor,
such as that of spices of various kinds, to a grateful
and pleasing perception, such as is that of truth
from good, or faith from charity.
Indeed the correspondence is such that in the other life,
whenever it is the good pleasure of the Lord,
perceptions themselves are changed into odors.*

—EMANUEL SWEDENBORG

Jonathan Edwards, the seventeenth-century revivalist preacher and theologian, described two types of gratitude in his classic work, *A Treatise Concerning Religious Affections.* He described these two types as natural gratitude and as a gracious or spiritual gratitude. Natural gratitude is thanks expressed to God for the benefits a person has received, whereas gracious gratitude has its source in the knowledge of the goodness of God independent of favors received. According to Edwards, the "gracious stirrings of grateful affection to God," in which love flows from the heart as a response to the Divine, is one of the surest ways to discern the presence of the Holy Spirit in a person's life.

Emanuel Swedenborg explained that angels in heaven perceived the gratefulness of worshipers as the sweet odor of incense, such as frankincense, and that this was received as prayer. This is also called the "prayer of saints" and explains

As the Father has loved me, so I have loved you;
Abide in my love. If you keep my commandments,
you will abide in my love, just as I have kept
my Father's commandments and abide in his love.
I have said these things to you so that my joy
may be in you, and that your joy may be complete.

—John 15:9–11

the meaning of the passage, "Let my prayer be counted as incense before you" (Psalm 141:2).

In response to questions from Pharisees about the greatest commandment, Jesus replied: "'You shall love the Lord your God with all your heart, and with all your soul, and with all your mind.' This is the greatest and first commandment. And a second is like it: 'You shall love your neighbor as yourself.' On these two commandments hang all the law and the prophets" (Matthew 22:37–40). These statements indicate both gratitude to our Creator and thankfulness to others demonstrated by our loving actions toward them.

ISLAM

The Holy Koran, which is divided into chapters called *suras,* repeatedly asserts the necessity for gratitude and thankfulness to God. For example, in Sura Fourteen it is written: "If you are grateful, I will give you more" (14:7). A traditional

SURA FATEHE

In the name of God,

Most gracious most merciful;

Praise be to God,

The cherisher and sustainer of the worlds;

Most gracious, most merciful;

Master of the day of judgment.

Thee do we worship, and Thine aid we seek.

(1 : 1—5)

Islamic saying states, "The first who will be summoned to paradise are those who have praised God in every circumstance." The prophet Muhammad also said, "Gratitude for the abundance you have received is the best insurance that the abundance will continue." True gratitude, it is taught, draws more abundant graces upon the believer.

The performance of the daily Islamic prayers is considered to be one of the "pillars" of the religion. The essence of the prayer is not to ask nor petition God, but to show everlasting praise and adoration to God for life and mercy.

Another pillar of Islam is fasting during the month of Ramadan. This period is intended to lead believers to a state of gratitude. "He wants you to complete the prescribed period and glorify him that He has guided you, and perchance ye shall be grateful" (Koran, 2:185).

In Sufism, the mystical tradition of Islam, entire book

It is love that brings happiness to people.

It is love that gives joy to happiness.

My mother didn't give birth to me, that love did.

A hundred blessings and praises to that love.

—RUMI

chapters have been devoted to developing gratitude. Different stages of gratitude are explained: the first is gratitude for the gifts received from God, as we would be grateful for any gift; a higher state is attained when one becomes grateful for not receiving gifts or for being delayed in having a hope fulfilled. In this state one sees the blessings that are veiled in affliction. The final state of gratitude is recognizing that no amount of worship is sufficient to express gratitude to the Creator and that even feelings of gratitude are a gift from God. There is gratitude for the capacity to feel grateful.

—— ✳ ——

These three religious perspectives contain within them the element of gratitude as an essential part of religious practice. The common thread is an overwhelming recognition of the

To speak gratitude is courteous and pleasant,
to enact gratitude is generous and noble,
but to live gratitude is to touch Heaven.

—JOHANNES A. GAERTNER

need always, in all circumstances, to remember the source from which we come. Sacred writings and prayers direct people to recognize their blessings and to demonstrate gratitude through their actions, their attitudes, and their prayers.

The greatest thing is to give thanks for everything.
He who has learned this knows what it means to live.
He has penetrated the whole mystery of life:
giving thanks for everything.

—ALBERT SCHWEITZER

CULTIVATING GRATITUDE

We can define what gratitude is and trace its importance throughout religious traditions over thousands of years. But how do we cultivate gratitude in our busy, event-filled lives? How can we bring this essential virtue into our daily experience?

As a way of bringing gratitude and the accompanying sense of thankfulness, joy, and well-being into our lives, we can explore several methods that have been developed for the purpose: one method is a conscious psychological tool; another is a personal, creative path of self-expression; the third method is a focused spiritual practice.

A hundred times a day I remind myself
that my inner and outer life depends
on the labors of other men,
living and dead,
and that I must exert myself in order
to give in the measure as I have received
and am still receiving.

—ALBERT EINSTEIN

The positive psychology movement not only identifies human strengths but also addresses the question of whether such human strengths can buffer people from psychological disorders. We can see that, according to classical writings and religious traditions, a grateful outlook does not require a life full of material comforts. Rather, an interior attitude of thankfulness can be sustained regardless of life circumstances.

This brings up several questions related to gratitude-centered interventions: Could depressed people profit from an exercise in thankfulness? Can the practice of gratitude alleviate distress as well as enhance positive well-being? What if destructive thoughts were redirected from self-inadequacy to undeserved merit? Might these serve as a buffer for people at risk for depression? Could gratitude be effective in reducing anger or other destructive emotions?

It is vital that people "count their blessings":
to appreciate what they possess
without having to undergo
its actual loss.

—ABRAHAM MASLOW

Psychologists have developed several methods to learn gratitude. One approach teaches the steps as: (1) identify non-grateful thoughts one has; (2) formulate gratitude-supporting thoughts; (3) substitute the grateful thoughts for the non-grateful ones; (4) translate the inner feelings to outward action.

Another method, based on taking a daily moral inventory, uses the feeling of gratitude to help people foster moral growth and a positive outlook on life. The first step in this method is to recognize that you are a moral person, a person of conscience. The next step is evoking gratitude for your blessings. Next, you conduct a self-examination of the day, then resolve to initiate some minimal behavioral change with the goal of increasing your moral maturity. Carrying out the self-examination in an authentic and meaningful way brings us to gratitude's key role. Assuming that you engage in a daily moral inventory with

*Gratitude is not only the greatest
of virtues,
but the parent
of all the others.*

—CICERO

the genuine intention of fostering personal moral growth, experiencing gratitude and the positive feeling states associated with it—such as humility and empathy toward others—will more than likely increase your sincerity and resolve. Gratitude might be considered a "buffer" that allays embarrassment, shame, or other negative emotions that might undermine self-honesty.

Though experienced for the most part as a pleasant affective state, a felt state of gratitude can require, at times, considerable effort. Events, people, or situations that are apt to evoke gratitude can easily be taken for granted or pushed aside as we contend with life's daily aggravations and struggle to regulate intense negative feelings. Nonetheless, making the personal commitment to invest psychic energy in developing a personal worldview of your life as a "gift" or as your very self as being "gifted" holds considerable importance from the standpoint of positive psychology. This idea also

Both abundance and lack exist simultaneously
in our lives, as parallel realities. It is always
our conscious choice which secret garden
we will tend . . . when we choose not to focus
on what is missing from our lives but are grateful
for the abundance that's present—
love, health, family, friends, work,
the joys of nature and personal pursuits
that bring us pleasure—
the wasteland of illusion falls away
and we experience Heaven on earth.

—SARAH BAN BREATHNACH

figures into the work and retreats of numerous religious groups, many of them influenced by the Jesuits, and in the practices of many self-help groups and organizations like Alcoholics Anonymous.

All in all, setting aside time on a daily basis to recall moments of gratitude associated with even mundane events, personal attributes, or valued people you encounter has the potential to infuse your life with cherished personal meaning just as it nourishes a fundamental positive life stance.

JOURNALING

Journaling is a centering practice; it keeps you still and focused while you write in a special notebook or journal for any number of reasons: self-expression, creative exploration, or as a catharsis for emotional pain. By listing those things for which we are grateful, we can be helped to grow in gratitude as we acknowledge God,

*Because gratification of a desire leads
to the temporary stilling of the mind
and the experience of the peaceful, joyful Self,
it's no wonder that we get hooked on thinking
that happiness comes from the satisfaction of desires.
This is the meaning of the old adage,
"Joy is not in things, it is in us."*

—JOAN BORYSENKO

friends, chance, love, fruitfulness, challenges, and insights.

What is helpful is to set aside time at the end of the day to sit quietly. Take ten minutes to quiet your mind, calm your thoughts, say a prayer if helpful, and simply let flow all the things that you appreciate in your life. Some practitioners suggest listing five or ten reasons why you are thankful, a simple practice. Another approach would be to let the feelings, joy, and thankfulness flow out of you— as poetry, prose, or artwork.

Take time to reflect on what you are feeling and thinking. Is this the first time that you have given thanks today? Or has your day become one of continuous thanksgiving? Has the habit of gratitude become yours?

If so, feel more gratitude.

If not, look at what made you forget to be grateful.

Let us rise up and be thankful,
for if we didn't learn a lot today,
at least we learned a little,
and if we didn't learn a little,
at least we didn't get sick,
and if we got sick,
at least we didn't die;
so, let us all be thankful.

—THE BUDDHA

As soon as you have assessed your feelings and understanding, begin to choose a way to give thanks. Simply by noticing five to ten things in your life that you are grateful for can change the way you perceive your world. What we pay attention to becomes our experience.

Sit quietly for a few minutes once you have finished. Notice your state of mind, breathing, and sensations. Journaling can be a very beneficial practice for certain people. It can help you get in touch with your mental habits and your emotional states.

BUDDHIST MEDITATION PRACTICE

A very helpful practice to cultivate gratitude is a Buddhist meditation technique called Naikan that was developed by Yoshimoto Ishin, a devout Buddhist from Japan and a member of the Jodo Shinshu sect. He developed the method as a way of helping others look inside, become introspective,

There is a calmness
to a life lived in Gratitude, a quiet joy.

—RALPH H. BLUM

and "see oneself with the mind's eye." The practice involves reflecting on three questions:

What have I received from _____?

What have I given to _____?

What troubles and difficulty have I _____?

These questions can help us address issues or relationships. They help us see the reciprocal quality of relationships and provide a structure for self-reflection. They can be directed toward work situations, toward social interactions, or toward developing higher aspects of oneself.

The first step or question involves recognizing all the gifts we receive. Remembering a person's smile, kind words, or helpful actions can elicit feelings of gratitude. When we focus on the good that comes to us every day, instead of being overwhelmed by the burden of our problems, we can be filled with deep appreciation.

*Man need only divert his attention from searching
for the solution to external questions and pose the one,
true inner question of how he should lead his life,
and all the external questions will be resolved
in the best possible way.*

—LEO TOLSTOY

Next we focus on what we give to others. This helps us realize how connected we are to other people and helps remove a sense of entitlement, that feeling that we are owed things from others and have no need to give back.

The last step is a difficult one: acknowledging not the things that bother us, but how we cause pain in the lives of others by our thoughts, words, and deeds. Greg Krech, who wrote on the practice of Naikan, says of this step, "If we are not willing to see and accept those events in which we have been the source of others' suffering, then we cannot truly know ourselves or the grace by which we live."

This practice of asking the three questions can be practiced each evening for about twenty minutes. It can be used to reflect on the day's activities in a general way. Another approach is to reflect on a specific relationship for fifty to sixty minutes. You can view a relationship

Thank God—
every morning when you get up—
that you have something to do which must be done,
whether you like it or not.
Being forced to work,
and forced to do your best, will breed in you
a hundred virtues which the idle never know.

—CHARLES KINGSLEY

chronologically or focus on a particular situation that might need attention.

A more intensive practice of Naikan takes place at weeklong retreats held at several centers in the United States. Retreat-goers do not make lists or write down their reflections: they sit in silent meditation as they look at a blank screen, replaying the story of their lives. These retreats produce profound results for the serious and sincere.

——— ❧❦❧ ———

It is helpful to look at different techniques of developing and experiencing gratitude. By learning and understanding these approaches, you can begin to create your own experiences and practices that help you get in touch with your own capability to open the door to appreciation for the gifts you are given.

Gratitude is the heart's memory.

—FRENCH PROVERB

RESEARCH AND RESULTS OF GRATITUDE

Psychologists have begun to look at certain behavior traits of people in an attempt to measure the possible effect these qualities would have on physical and emotional health. In relation to gratitude, our research group wondered if an intentional grateful focus, practiced on a sustained basis, could have a measurable beneficial effect on health and well-being. While a person cannot simply choose to "be grateful," he or she can learn to focus on the benefits that are all around us that will lead to the feeling of gratitude.

It has long been assumed that an effective strategy for enhancing one's emotional life is to count one's blessings.

Develop an attitude of gratitude,
and give thanks for everything
that happens to you,
knowing that every step forward
is a step toward achieving
something bigger and better
than your current situation.

—BRIAN TRACY

Recent research conducted in our laboratory in the psychology department at the University of California, Davis, provides an empirical test of this assertion. In our journaling studies, participants are randomly assigned to one of three conditions. One-third of the research participants are asked to put in writing up to five major events or circumstances that affected them. Another third are asked to write down five hassles or minor stressors. The final third are asked to write down five things for which they are grateful or thankful. In a variation on this procedure, we ask one group to focus on ways in which they think they are better off than others. We have asked participants to do this either on a weekly or a daily basis for periods ranging from two to ten weeks. During this time they also keep logs of their moods, energy levels, health behaviors, pain, and physical complaints.

Gratitude is something of which
none of us can give too much.
For on the smiles, the thanks we give,
our little gestures of appreciation,
our neighbors build their philosophy of life.

—A. J. CRONIN

Results indicate significant differences between the groups. Compared to the hassles and events groups, participants in the gratitude groups felt better about their lives as a whole, they felt more alive and energetic, and they were more optimistic concerning the upcoming week. They reported fewer physical complaints and spent more time exercising than did the subjects in the other two groups. In a second study, the group with a gratitude focus reported higher levels of alertness and energy compared to those focusing on hassles or to those participants who focused on how they were better off than others. Those in the gratitude group were also more likely to report helping someone with a personal problem or offering emotional support to another, suggesting that positive social behavior is a consequence of being grateful. Not only did they feel good, they also did good.

One can never pay in gratitude:
One can only "pay in kind" somewhere else in life.

— ANNE MORROW LINDBERGH

Somewhat surprisingly, we did not find that the practice of gratitude buffered individuals from the experience of unpleasant emotions. Gratefulness does not appear to be a Pollyannaish state where suffering and adversity are selectively ignored. It may, however, help practitioners develop the necessary psychological resources to successfully weather unpleasant emotional states.

Additionally, scores on a questionnaire developed by Southern Methodist University psychologist Michael McCullough to measure gratefulness as a personality trait were positively associated with frequency of engaging in altruistic activities like volunteering, tutoring, and donating money to worthy causes. Questionnaire results also demonstrated that grateful individuals place less importance on material goods; they are less likely to judge their own and others' success in terms of possessions accumulated. Other researchers have actually

He is a wise man who does not grieve
for the things which he has not,
but rejoices for those which he has.

—Epictetus

shown that grateful individuals may live longer than those less grateful.

Why does gratitude work? A grateful response to life circumstances may be an adaptive psychological strategy and an important process by which people positively interpret everyday experiences. Focusing on the gifts one has been given is an antidote to envy, resentment, regret, and other negative states that undermine long-term happiness. The experience of gratitude, and the actions stimulated by it, also build and strengthen social bonds and friendships. Encouraging people to focus on the benefits they have received from others leads them to feel loved and cared for, and perceived social support is vital to physical and psychological health. We are engaged in further studies designed to explore the healing power of gratitude and to examine how the conscious cultivation of gratitude can create an upward spiral of health, wholeness, and goodness.

A proud man is seldom a grateful man,

for he never thinks he gets as much as he deserves.

—HENRY WARD BEECHER

HINDRANCES TO GRATITUDE

What personality traits are the greatest impediments to that overwhelming, joyful feeling of gratitude and thanksgiving? What qualities do we need to look for, in ourselves and in others, that might indicate why gratitude could be an elusive experience for some people?

Some personality and behavioral traits block a person from experiencing gratitude and encourage a sense of ingratitude. The ungrateful person appears to display a personality that manifests narcissistic tendencies. Narcissism is characterized by a sense of excessive self-importance, arrogance, vanity, and need for admiration and entitlement. People who exhibit

Gratitude is a sickness suffered by dogs.

—JOSEPH STALIN

these traits believe they are entitled to special rights and privileges, whether earned or not.

Narcissistic personalities tend to be demanding and selfish. They possess an exaggerated sense of deserving and expect special favors without assuming reciprocal responsibilities; in fact, they will express surprise and anger when others do not do what they want. The sense of entitlement combined with a lack of sensitivity to the needs of others results in selfish behavior on their part. Simply stated, if one is entitled to everything, then one is thankful for nothing.

Based on clinical observations, psychologists have noted that narcissists are incapable of experiencing and expressing sincere gratitude toward others. Narcissism is a spiritual blindness; it is a refusal to acknowledge that one has been the recipient of benefits freely bestowed by others.

This information is helpful to someone who is trying to develop the virtue of gratitude in his or her own life. When

It is another's fault if he be ungrateful,

but is mine if I do not give.

To find one thankful man,

I will oblige a great many that are not so.

—SENECA

some of these negative personality traits emerge in ourselves and others or if we are questioning why we cannot feel grateful at certain times, it would be beneficial to see if we can find our own behavior on the entitlement side of the balance sheet.

With this information, we can also learn to be more sensitive to others and more humble in our actions and attitudes. Knowing what the hindrances to gratitude are can serve a very vital function of making us aware of our own roadblocks to feeling joy and peace in our lives. It will also help us to become more compassionate to the suffering of others who might be caught in the trap of vanity and greed. They are denying themselves one of the greatest gifts available, the gift of love—given and received.

If the only prayer you ever say
in your entire life is "thank you,"
it will be enough.

—Meister Eckhardt

PRAYING FOR GRATITUDE

The words seem so easy: be grateful and you will be filled with joy, happiness, and a sense of fulfillment. According to some interpretations, you will even be in heaven. Simply open your heart and mind to the glories of the universe and the infinite blessings that shower upon us and you will live in the heavenly sphere of gratitude. If it is so easy in theory, then why is it so hard in actuality? What keeps us from giving thanks at all times in all situations? What can we do to pull ourselves out of a state of deprivation and resentment?

We have become aware that entitlement can block the process, as can the feeling of being a victim. When we fall

Lord, you came to give us life,
And life that was more abundant.
Help me not to run away from life,
But to follow your spirit,
To accept the thorn
As well as the flower
And to be grateful
For the gift of life.

—FRANK TOPPING

into the trap of blaming other people rather than taking responsibility for the challenges we face, solving a problem or being grateful for the solution becomes more difficult. It takes a big leap of faith or courage to see sufferings as blessings. It seems almost beyond comprehension when we read that Helen Keller believed her considerable handicaps to be among the greatest blessings in her life. She wrote, "I have never believed that my limitations were in any sense punishments or accidents. If I had held such a view, I could never have exerted the strength to overcome them. I thank God for my handicaps; for through them, I have found myself, my work, and my God."

Being ungrateful can also be related to being overly materialistic—thinking happiness comes from things rather than from within. We may feel ungrateful or cheated when we look at what others have that we think is missing in our own lives—loving relationships, wealth, material possessions,

How shall I repay your generosity, O my Lover?
How shall I repay you for all you have given me?
If I had died a thousand times for your sake,
it would be as nothing. . . .
How shall I thank you, who suffered dishonor,
insult, mockery, scourging, and death for my sake? . . .
The only thing I can return to you is my prayer,
that time I devote each day
speaking and listening to you.
Receive my prayer, as a tiny token
of my enormous gratitude.

—TYCHON OF ZADONSK

supportive family. We can get caught up with wanting what others have and can experience the emotions of envy and greed.

One of the greatest obstacles to experiencing the fullness and joy of life is simply that we do not take the time to reflect on our blessings. With the distractions of our responsibilities and material needs, the quiet time for reflection disappears. A conscious feeling of resentment or deprivation does not keep us from this experience; rather, a lack of awareness, or living in an unconscious sleep state of not being thankful, does so.

Attending regular religious services, meditating, and praying all help to remind us of our deeper, connected selves. Although a disciplined practice can encourage feelings of gratitude and thankfulness, we can incorporate prayer or quiet times of contemplation into our daily, active lives in other ways. Every act can be one of thankfulness: every

Everything is, is freely given by the God of love.
All is grace.
Light and water, shelter and food, work and free time,
children, parents, grandparents, life and death—
it is all given to us.
Why? So that we can say thanks:
thanks to God, thanks to each other,
thanks to all and everyone.

—HENRI NOUWEN

dish we wash, memo we write, lawn we mow, can be given in thanks for the gifts of food, work, and shelter.

Prayers also help to remind us of our gifts. If we cannot pray from a sense of gratitude, we can pray to experience that feeling. Prayer is, in fact, being open to the Divine inspiration that is available to us at all times. When we ask for this help in times of need, we will receive it—not always in the way we think we might deserve, but the gift is there nonetheless. If we cannot recognize it, we can pray for the help to see, feel, smell, or sense the overpowering love that surrounds us all. We are like radio or television sets. The airways are carrying all types of messages; we just have to turn on the receiver and tune in the right channel.

Brother David Steindl-Rast asks an important question in his essay, "Are You Thankful or Are You Grateful?" He talks about the gratitude that overwhelms a person who loses sense of self in wonder—when time and space are suspended—such

Grant me, O Lord,

to know what I ought to know,

to love what I ought to love,

to praise what delights you most,

to value what is precious in your sight,

to hate what is offensive to you.

Do not allow me to judge according to the sight of my eyes,

nor to pass sentence according to the hearing

of the ears of ignorant men;

but to discern with a true judgment between things visible

and spiritual, and above all things, always to inquire

what is the good pleasure of your will.

—SAINT THOMAS À KEMPIS

as being overcome by the majesty of the night sky. The next response would be a conscious reflection of the beauty of the event and a sense of thankfulness. He says, "Gratefulness turns into thankfulness. This is a different fullness. A moment ago you were fully aware; now you are thoughtful. Gratefulness is full awareness; thankfulness is thoughtfulness."

Being grateful is being the gift, giver, and receiver at once. He goes on to explain that "gratefulness is the mystical dimension of gratitude; thankfulness is its theological one."

We can go through the motions of being thankful, with the help of religious instruction or organized services such as grace before meals. However, the shift to gratitude comes from the inside moving from the external display, no matter how sincere or not, to an internal resonance with the Divine. The shift is accompanied by a sense of being part of something greater, of being carried along and lifted up on a wave of expansion, awareness, and gratitude. This can happen

IRISH PRAYER

May there always be work
for your hands to do
May your purse always hold
a coin or two
May the sun always shine
on your window pane
May a rainbow be certain
to follow each rain
May the hand of a friend always
be near you and
May God fill your heart
with gladness to cheer you.

in a flash or can come after reflection, meditation, and prayer. The experience is what fills our thankfulness and makes it sincere.

We have learned from the research that grateful people elicit more support from others. They cope better, have better health, and are more socially adaptable. This strong data supports grateful behavior. The key is learning how to make it part of our experience.

When we feel unhappy and upset about life, we are tempted to go through the hypocritical motions of candy-coating our experiences, making "lemonade out of lemons." This can often shortcut the process of self-inquiry that will lead to genuine understanding. Instead, it might be a good time to go ahead and feel the bitterness of your pain to allow genuine and honest feelings to emerge. Feel your feelings as they are, not through rose-colored glasses, opening the door to authentic spiritual growth.

Gratitude is vital for each of us
if we are to understand ourselves;
for gratitude sees, and fully affirms,
our dependency, our lack,
our need to receive all that
which we cannot provide for ourselves.

—BALDUIN SCHWARZ

From that space of honesty, ask for help. Ask to have your heart opened to feel the gifts that are being showered upon you. Ask for light to fill your darkness. Ask for sweetness in place of sorrow. Ask to choose the way of an open heart rather than a broken one. Above all, be truthful. Do not rationalize, justify, or make excuses. Open your heart to genuine truth and love.

Know that the world and your experience becomes whatever you turn your attention to. Take responsibility for turning your thoughts upward, to your highest expression. Pray for the guidance to live in the recognition of the source of all good and truth. Know that with this knowledge will come a love of truth and the wisdom of love. Know that you will bask in the warmth and the light of a blessed state, gratitude.

To help with this process, find prayers, or use the ones provided here to put yourself in a receptive state. As we order

*Let the words of my mouth
and the meditations of my heart
be pleasing to you,
O Lord,
my rock and my redeemer.*

—PSALM 19

our external lives, we will provide a safe receptacle for the internal flowing in of Divine love. As this begins to happen in our lives, the responsibility we have to make it real is to give it to others in words and deeds. As this love and wisdom filter into your attitudes and actions, you will find yourself more loving to others and more loved. You will attract goodness and good people into your life as your gratitude turns into actions.

THE SECRET

I met God in the morning
When my day was at its best,
And His presence came like sunrise,
Like a glory in my breast.
All day long the Presence lingered,
All day long He stayed with me,
And we sailed in perfect calmness
O'er a very troubled sea.
Other ships were blown and battered,
Other ships were sore distressed,

But the winds that seemed to drive them
Brought to us a peace and rest.
Then I thought of other mornings,
With a keen remorse of mind,
When I too had loosed the moorings,
With the Presence left behind.
So I think I know the secret,
Learned from many a troubled way;
You must seek Him in the morning
If you want him through the day!

—RALPH SPAULDING CUSHMAN

WHAT GOD IS LIKE

I did not know what God is like
Until a friendly word
Came to me in an hour of need—
And it was God I heard.
I did not know what God is like
Until I heard love's feet
On errands of God's mercy
Go up and down life's street.

I did not know what God is like
Until I felt a hand
Clasp mine and lift me when alone
I had no strength to stand.
I think I know what God is like
For I have seen the face
Of God's son looking at me
From all the human race.

— JAMES DILLET FREEMAN

GOD SPOKE TO ME

Through the song of a bird

He announced His presence.

Through a golden sunrise

He shared some of His splendor.

Through a season of silence

He called me His child.

Through His word of Truth

He told me the Way.

Through the smile of a friend
He revealed His nature.
Through the eyes of an infant
He expressed His joy.
Through the sparkle of raindrops
He spoke of a miracle.
Through my time of indecision
He gave me the answer.

—WILLIAM ARTHUR WARD

THE LARGER PRAYER

At first I prayed for Light:
Could I but see the way,
How gladly, swiftly would I walk
To everlasting day!
And next I prayed for Strength:
That I might tread the road
With firm, unfaltering feet, and win
The heaven's serene abode.
And then I asked for Faith:
Could I but trust my God,
I'd live enfolded in His peace,
Though foes were all abroad.

But now I pray for Love:
Deep love to God and man,
A living love that will not fail,
However dark His plan.
And Light and Strength and Faith
Are opening everywhere;
God only waited for me, till
I prayed the larger prayer.

—EDNAH D. CHENEY

*We are created to share
in God's love and life for eternity.
The experience of this love
is manifested in our response
of praise, reverence and service,
that is, loving God with all our heart,
all our mind and all our will.*

—IGNATIUS LOYOLA

REFERENCES
AND FURTHER READING

Danner, D., D.A. Snowden, and W.F. Friesen. 2001. Positive emotions in early life and longevity: Findings from the Nun study. *Journal of Personality and Social Psychology,* 80:804–813.

Emmons, R.A., and C.A. Crumpler. 2000. Gratitude as human strength: Appraising the evidence. *Journal of Social and Clinical Psychology* 19:56–69.

Emmons, R.A., and M.E. McCullough. 2001. *Counting blessings versus burdens: An experimental investigation of gratitude and subjective well-being in daily life.* Manuscript submitted for publication.

Keller, Helen. 1927. Revision 1994 by R. Silverman. *Light in my darkness.* West Chester, Penna: Chrysalis Books.

McCullough, M.E., R.A. Emmons, and J. Tsang. In press. The grateful disposition: A conceptual and empirical topography. *Journal of Personality and Social Psychology*.

McCullough, M.E., S. Kirkpatrick, R.A. Emmons and D. Larson. 2001. Is gratitude a moral affect? *Psychological Bulletin* 127:249–266.

Swedenborg, Emanuel. 1998. Translated by J. Clowes; revised and edited by J.F. Potts *Arcana coelestia*. West Chester, Penna: Swedenborg Foundation.

WEBSITES

www.anamorph.com/todo

www.beliefnet.com

www.gratefulness.org

www.spirituality.com

www.templeton.org

www.templetonpress.org

www.thanksgiving.org

SUGGESTED READINGS

Brussat, F., and M.A. Brussat. 2000. *Spiritual Rx: Prescriptions for living a meaningful life.* New York: Hyperion.

Carman, J.B., and F.J. Streng, eds. 1989. *Spoken and unspoken thanks: Some comparative soundings.* Dallas, Tex.: Center for World Thanksgiving.

Goodenough, U. 1998. *The sacred depths of nature.* New York: Oxford University Press.

Miller, T. 1995. *How to want what you have.* New York: Avon.

Ryan, M.J. 1999. *Attitudes of gratitude: How to give and receive joy every day of your life.* Berkeley, Calif.: Conari Press

Steindl-Rast, D. 1984. *Gratefulness, the heart of prayer.* New York: Paulist.

ACKNOWLEDGMENTS

From *Rending the Veil: Literal and Poetic Translations of Rumi* by Shahram T. Shiva. (Prescott, AZ: Holm Press, 1995). Used by permission.

"What God Is Like," from *What God Is Like* (1973). Used with permission of Unity School of Christianity, 1901 NW Blue Parkway, Unity Village, MO 64065.

"God Spoke to Me," from *Truth the Poet Sings* (1984). Used with permission of Unity School of Christianity, 1901 NW Blue Parkway, Unity Village, MO 64065.